MOSES THE TRAV[illegible]ER

GUIDE[illegible]

BOOK 4 (TOLD FROM[illegible]

CARINE MACKENZIE

Illustrated by

Graham Kennedy

Published by Christian Focus Publications,

Geanies House, Fearn, Tain, Ross-shire, IV20 1TW, Scotland, U.K.

www.christianfocus.com

Printed in China

God rescued his people, the Hebrews, from slavery in Egypt. They reached the Red Sea. Pharaoh's soldiers chased after them. They were so afraid. They were trapped – sea in front, soldiers behind.

They complained to Moses. "You have taken us here to die in the desert."

"Do not be afraid," said Moses, "Stand firm and see the salvation of the Lord."

God told Moses to hold out his staff towards the Red Sea. The Lord drove the sea back by a strong east wind, leaving a path across to the other side. Moses led the people across.

The Egyptian soldiers tried to follow but the chariot wheels got stuck. God told Moses to stretch out his hand over the sea. The water came crashing back, drowning the Egyptians.

The people feared the Lord and believed in him.

After walking for three days the people were desperate for water. At last they found some at Marah. But when they tasted it, it was bitter and nasty. The people complained to Moses. God showed Moses a tree. He threw the tree into the water. God made the water sweet and drinkable.

"If you listen to me and obey my words," God told them, "I will look after you for I am the Lord who heals you."

God still provides our food and drink. Everything we need comes from him.

The people complained to Moses again.

"We used to have plenty to eat in Egypt. Now we are so hungry."

God spoke to Moses, "I have heard the people's complaints." He promised to give them food.

That evening the camp was covered with lots of little birds called quails. The Hebrew people had plenty of meat to eat.

Do you remember to thank God for what he gives you to eat?

God provided special bread too. In the morning the ground was covered with little white seeds which looked like dew drops. They called it manna. Each family collected what they needed for that day.

On the sixth day of the week they collected twice as much, some to use on the Sabbath because God did not send manna on the Sabbath.

God provided this food for all the years that the Hebrew people were travelling in the desert.

They travelled on and still they complained. "We have no water here."

God spoke to Moses. "Take your rod with you. Speak to that rock and it will let out water for you."

Moses stood in front of the rock as the people watched. Moses spoke angrily to the people and hit the rock twice with his rod. Water came rushing out.

God provided for his people. But he was displeased that Moses had not obeyed him exactly.

Moses' father-in-law, Jethro, heard news of Moses and all that God had done for him and the people. He came to visit Moses in the desert. When he saw how hard he was working, settling disputes and making judgements, he gave him good advice.

"You will wear yourself out. Get others to help you. Choose able, truthful men and train them to make decisions. When a difficult case comes up, you can deal with that."

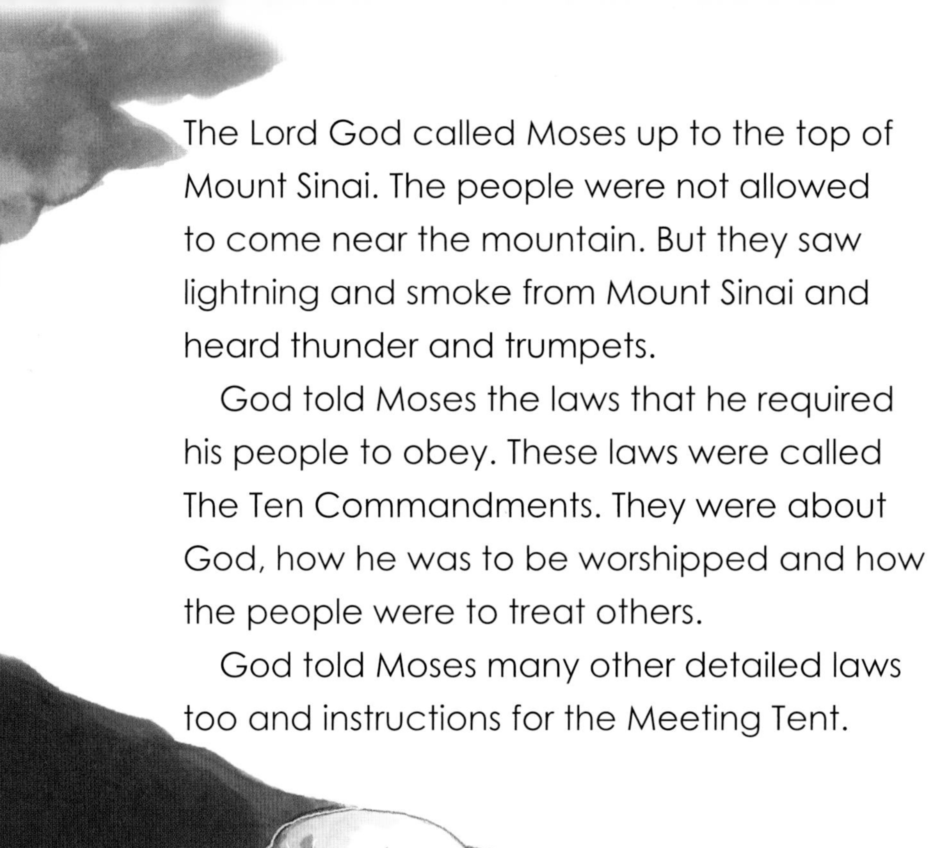

The Lord God called Moses up to the top of Mount Sinai. The people were not allowed to come near the mountain. But they saw lightning and smoke from Mount Sinai and heard thunder and trumpets.

God told Moses the laws that he required his people to obey. These laws were called The Ten Commandments. They were about God, how he was to be worshipped and how the people were to treat others.

God told Moses many other detailed laws too and instructions for the Meeting Tent.

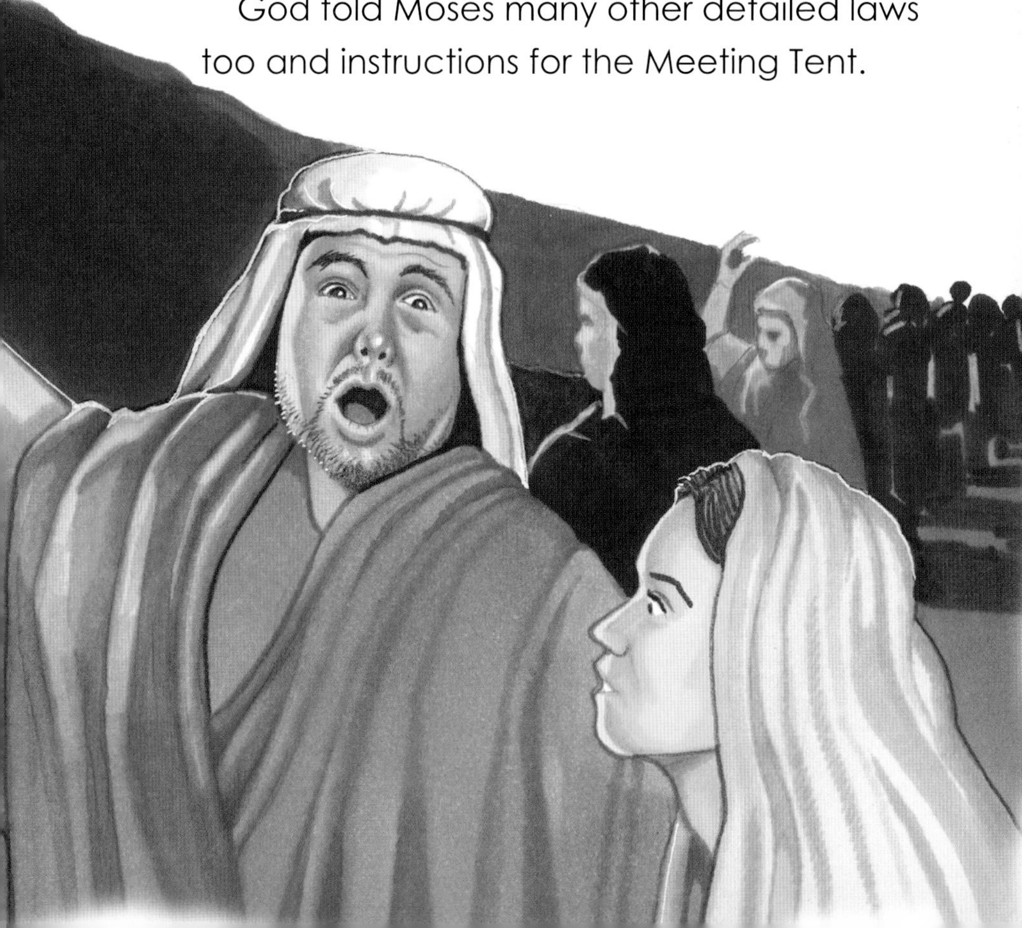

After God had finished speaking with Moses, he gave him two tablets of stone with the commandments written on them.

The people became impatient when Moses was away for so long, forty days and nights.

"Make us a golden idol to worship," they asked Aaron. Foolishly he agreed, collected gold jewellery and melted it together and made a golden calf.

When Moses came down, he saw what was happening. He was so angry, he threw down the stone tablets which broke in pieces.

Moses returned to meet with God and humbly confessed the people's sins to God. God punished them, but he heard Moses' prayers for forgiveness and mercy.

"My presence will go with you," God said, "And I will give you rest."

God instructed Moses to cut two new tablets of stone, like the first ones.

Early in the morning Moses climbed Mount Sinai again alone. God descended in a cloud.

Moses bowed down to worship. God again wrote the Ten Commandments on the stones.

We can read these Ten Commandments in the Bible. God has given them to us to obey.

At last the people reached the land of Canaan that God had promised to give them.

Moses looked over the land from the top of Mount Nebo but he was not allowed to enter.

Moses was 120 years old when he died. The people mourned and wept for thirty days.

For forty years Moses and the people wandered in the desert, camping in different places. The people were often discontented and sinned. Even Moses sinned. God had to punish sin but he showed mercy and forgiveness.

Our sin deserves God's punishment too. The Lord Jesus Christ came to die on the cross at Calvary to pay the price for the sins of those who trust in him.